The Villa

From Ancient to Modern

The Villa

From Ancient to Modern

By Joseph Rykwert

Photographs by Roberto Schezen

Harry N. Abrams, Inc., Publishers

Project manager: Diana Murphy
Editor: Julia Gaviria
Designer: Judith Hudson

*Pages 2–3: Giacomo da Vignola, Villa Lante, view of
the upper garden; 4–5: Gwathmey Siegel & Associates
Architects, François de Menil House, southeast view*

Library of Congress Cataloging-in-Publication Data
Rykwert, Joseph, 1926–
The villa: from ancient to modern / by Joseph Rykwert ;
photographs by Roberto Schezen.
      p.   cm.
Includes index.
ISBN 0–8109–3944–4 (hardcover)
1. Architecture, Domestic—Europe. 2. Historic build-
ings—Europe. 3. Architecture, Domestic—United States.
4. Historic buildings—United States. I. Schezen,
Roberto. II. Title.

NA7580 .R94 2000
728.8'09182'1—dc21   00–22799

Printed and bound in Japan

Harry N. Abrams, Inc.
100 Fifth Avenue
New York, N.Y. 10011
www.abramsbooks.com

Contents

The Villa

Andare in villegiatura – to go a-village-ing – has come to mean to go on vacation to modern Italians. Whether traveling to the sea or up into the mountains – or just into the country – it is all *villegiatura* to them, and suggests a cool, airy house, a break from the pressures and anxieties of life in town – a holiday, in short. That image of the countryside offering respite from the dirty, polluted, crowded, and aggressive city has existed since Roman antiquity. It is implied by the first writers in Latin on country matters: the great general and orator, Cato, and the prolific scholar (and when he wrote on agriculture, very aged, but chatty) Varro; Virgil, in the *Georgics,* produced a verse treatise about the pleasures of country life; the satirists, beginning with Horace, rather go on about it. The busy lawyer and politician Pliny the Younger, a friend of the emperor Trajan, writes in a reproachful letter to his all-too-relaxed country-loving friend Praesens:

Will you never change your country dress for the habit of the town . . . it is time . . . for you to revisit our scene of bustle, were it only that your rural pleasures may not grow languid by enjoyment: appear at the levees of the great that you may enjoy the same honor yourself with more satisfaction; and mix in the crowd that you may have a stronger relish for the charms of solitude. [1]

Pliny the Younger was called that to distinguish him from his equally famous uncle and adopted father, Pliny the Elder, who had written the ency-clopedic *Natural History* and was suffocated by the fumes of the great volcanic eruption of Vesuvius in AD 79. For all his reproaches to Praesens, Pliny owned several villas himself, though in his letters, which were certainly meant for publication, he writes mostly about his two preferred houses, the Laurentine on the seaside (not far from the mouth of the Tiber), and the Tuscan in the hills near the modern Città di Castello, east of Arezzo. His letters provide much detail about the landscape, which "preserves its verdure perfectly well," and his gardens with "a terrace perfumed with violets and warmed by the reflection of the sun"; the quality of the Laurentine coast is such that "what part soever you dig you meet . . . with a spring of pure water," while the sea there produces "very extraordinary fish."

These are villas quite different from those built in the early days of the Republic, when a noble Roman would cultivate his own land, perhaps with the help of a few slaves. The legend of Cincinnatus, the "curly one," made him an exemplar of ancient virtue. He was called from the field he was ploughing (near the Vatican, perhaps) to become dictator of Rome when it was threatened by the Samnites in 458 BC. Having saved the city, he returned to his plough sixteen days later and without regret. Cato the Censor (his official title, which suited his crabby personality) could still write that to call a man a good husbandman was the highest compliment, and the neglect of land was a punishable offense.

1. Pliny the Younger, *The Letters,* translated by William Melmoth (London, 1747; modified), Book VII, Letter 3.

But already in Cato's lifetime, in the second century BC, the territorial expansion of Rome was modifying rural life. Imported cheap Sicilian (and later African) grain meant that oil, vines, vegetable gardens, and cattle were becoming the profitable "home" produce. Small holdings where the land was tilled by a citizen owner were disappearing. Three or four generations later, Varro considered that an owner (whom he limited to some 160 acres) needed a twin or double house, a *villa urbana* for himself and a *villa rustica* for his bailiff, slaves, and employees as well as for machinery – milling, oil and wine presses, and storage. The villa at Boscoreale, about a mile from Pompeii, is organized in that way.

At the end of the Republican period, there was a great deal of money about. Relatively small holdings were absorbed into ever larger *latifundia*, semi-industrial farming estates. Buildings had to be organized for larger slave and employee quarters. Increasingly, therefore, capital investment in farming led to the creation of a wealthy and influential class of Roman patricians with much land but little or no personal involvement in farming. They were probably the first Romans to build villas in which relaxation – *otium,* leisure, the opposite of *negotium,* business – was the prime consideration.

Cato had begun his treatise *De Re Rustica* – which is one of the earliest Latin prose books to have survived – with advice on the best position for a villa. His farmer only occupied a single house, facing south if possible, near a river, at the foot of a hill, close to vineyards, woods, and fields. Columella (from Cadiz, though he seems to have owned some land in Italy) wrote three hundred years later, at the time of the emperor Tiberius, and had similar ideas about siting, though, as a professional farmer,

he preferred the plains and an east-facing position. He suggests, too, that there should be three kinds of villas on an estate: *urbana,* for the owner; *rustica,* for the bailiff, slaves, and the kitchens; and *fructuaria,* for the orchards. We know more about what went on inside the rustic villa from the architectural treatise of Vitruvius, *De Architectura,* which was the first architectural book; he seems to have been quite old when he dedicated it to Octavian Augustus, which makes him contemporary with Varro. Vitruvius outlines all the different apartments that a *villa rustica* must have versus those of a *villa urbana.* The rustic house, he insists, must be light, which is easier to arrange in the country than in town, and he offers a good deal of country wisdom about cattle being made to face the east and being fed standing toward the sun (which will give a good gloss to their skins); he knows that baths (for people returning from work in the fields) must be near the entrance, but also near the kitchen since both places are hot and need a water supply. He is explicit about cowsheds and how sheep and goats should be accommodated around a court, and how granaries as well as cellars for oil and wine storage should be arranged to avoid the danger of fire. Additional rooms, he advises, are required for slaves and retainers. All this agrees with Varro.

As for the parts of the main house, he seems to assume that they will be much the same as those in the town house: a porter's lodge, followed by a narrow passage into the atrium, a darkish space (*atrium,* from *ater,* smoky, dark – nothing to do with the glazed foyers of our hotels), with the seat of the *paterfamilias* and the altars of the household gods. On either side of the *atrium* are private rooms and the *alae,* the wings where ancestral portraits are kept, and beyond it a peristyle colonnade and the *triclinium,* the "best" dining room, which Cato wants to face west but Vitruvius prefers on the north. Vitruvius also indicates the perfect proportions of rooms, whether square or oblong, and the position and use of the different parts of the house. As is clear from the Villa of the Mysteries in Pompeii, an interior courtyard was very much a feature of the larger villa.

Pliny and Vitruvius provide much information about how villas were occupied, but little was actually known about them until two centuries ago, when a happy accident led to the discovery of the ruins of Herculaneum and Pompeii, the two towns that had been prosperous country towns as well as seaside resorts and were buried in the ash and lava produced by the great and wholly unexpected explosion of Vesuvius in AD 79, the same one that killed Pliny the Elder. As house after house was discovered, many of them were reconstructed, and in some their furniture as well as metal objects, even a whole library, in one case, were recovered. And of course in many of them a great deal of the decoration, some in plaster relief, and much of it painted, had survived.

About the most splendid decorations were those in the suburban Villa of the Mysteries. It seems to have changed ownership after an earthquake in AD 62, though its original owners had made the villa very splendid. Herculaneum and Pompeii have offered, because of their sudden destruction, precious evidence about how such country houses were used; in other places villas were occupied over several generations, and each owner destroyed the evidence left by his predecessors.

Throughout Imperial times, until the late fourth century, the villa was the resort of the prosperous Roman. Since all transport was on horseback or on foot, a villa could not be located too far out of town. Those who could not walk or ride long distances could travel by litter or, exceptionally, by wagon or chariot, which, not being sprung, would be very uncomfortable. At any rate a "weekend in deep country" was not conceivable if it took you a whole day to get there. The villa either had to be within easy reach of town or of another type, equipped, as Pliny's were, to accommodate the owners and their guests for weeks or even months. Prosperous Romans had a number of favorite spots – the Tuscan hills and the seaside near Naples – which were all crowded with villas, as were the hills inland just south of Rome, at Tusculum, for instance, where Cicero lived, and where he held his famous philosophical disputations. Emperors built villas for private entertainment, as Tiberius did on a promontory on the Isle of Capri. Not far from Tusculum, on the plain below the hill town of Tibur (now Tivoli, and the site of some spectacular villas), the emperor Hadrian built himself the one that must be the acme of all villa building in the ancient world.

The Romans built villas not just in the preferred spots mentioned above but all over their empire, from Egypt to Britain. Besides Hadrian's in Tivoli, about the most splendid to survive is the rather mysterious "imperial" villa at Piazza Armerina in the east of Sicily, just off the Catania–Agrigento road, and the center of a prosperous farming estate. Although it was damaged by the Goths, it survived, rather dilapidated, into the Arab and Byzantine period, to be wrecked finally in the twelfth century by a violent flood. But the villa at Piazza Armerina, with its oval peristyles and extravagant floor mosaics, was already out of its time. Living in a villa and enjoying its amenities is only possible in peaceful times, when policing is relatively effective. As conditions became unsettled with the fall of the empire in the West, the villas became fortresses, and even castles. The last emperor of the West, ironically called Romulus Augustulus (uniting the name of the founder of Rome and the first emperor), was "retired" in 476 by the Ostrogothic ruler Odoacer to the villa that the dictator Marius had built for himself at Cape Misenum just north of Naples, over-looking the bay. It had been rebuilt by Lucullus – whose name is a byword for luxury – though by this time it was called a castle and had been fortified. It was then turned into a monastery and was finally pulled down about the break of the millennium.

That is where Western Europeans who wanted country life and *otium* retired between 500 and 1400: to a monastery. Castles were really places of *negotium*, war and administration. The monastery offered a life of work in agriculture but also leisure for prayer. Leisure was harder to come by in the north than in the south. Several rulers – notably the Norman kings ruling their eclectic, Greco-Moorish courts from Palermo (particularly William I and II, r. 1154–66, 1171–89, respectively) – built themselves Arab-style park-pavilions, "La Zisa" and "La Cuba," using Moorish masons from their remaining lands in Tunisia. Other southern rulers were also keen to return to some form of relaxed, suburban exis-tence. Yet when the emperor Frederick II built the famous Castel del Monte in Puglia, between 1240 and 1250, it was hardly a medieval villa but more like a castle that could not be defended, even if it had been intended as a hunting lodge (Frederick was an enthusiastic falconer). After his death it was used as a prison and as a bandits' lair – and stripped of its sculptures and decorations. In the Middle Ages country houses were in fact rarely more than hunting lodges, and were camped in rather than fully occupied if they were built at all.

While that state of affairs subsisted in Christian Europe, the Arab rulers of North Africa and Spain had established their hegemony over the western Mediterranean. The Spanish courts, in Granada especially, had developed a light and entrancing way of building: they crowned fortified emplace-ments with pavilioned pleasure gardens in which water and shade were artificiously disposed in room and courtyard sequences for maximum gratification. Only the Sicilian Normans managed to emulate the Moors convincingly.

The situation changed in the West between 1300 and 1400. When Boccaccio's young people escaping from the plague outbreak of 1348 gathered in an abandoned, porticoed, and frescoed country house a mere two miles out of Florence, their storytelling, which turned into the *Decameron,* invoked the *otium* of the ancient villa. Bubonic plague, the Black Death, which hit Europe very hard at midcentury, changed much in Europe. Its withdrawal, as incom-prehensible as its coming, led to an economic revival and a keen reassessment of the structure of author-ity. Financial power was gaining at the expense of the political, which led to a demand for greater security. The example of antiquity in the arts, but also in economy and administration, created a new yearning for an antique-style way of doing things, and above all, for antique-style building. At the same time, the devising and perfecting of artillery led to a shift in the conduct of warfare and the restructuring of defensive walls.

Cities extended their writ into the country. In Florence, whose nobility (unlike nobility farther north or in Iberia) was involved in commerce and banking, leading families would build themselves villas in the ancient sense, that is, associated with a farming enterprise, as the Medici did at Poggio a Caiano. Yet they would still visit monasteries for a taste of country life, as Lorenzo de' Medici (the Magnificent) would go up to Camaldoli in the hills above Florence, where he patronized philosophical disputations on the model of Cicero's Tusculan conversations. On the other side of the country, as the Venetian Republic extended its rule over the mainland and its commerce was threatened by the new transatlantic navigation, its patriciate bought into the rich farmland in the Po valley and turned themselves into gentlemen-farmers. The papacy, too, asserted its rule over the surroundings of Rome, although banditism was not finally put down until the fierce and highly efficient Sixtus V (r. 1590–95). Many Roman magnates were building villas even before his time, mostly in the southern zone, the Castelli Romani: at Tivoli, where they could do so within the walls, and at Frascati. Those who could afford private policing ventured more to the north: Bagnaia, Caprarola, Bracciano.

Still later the hunting lodges of the French kings would turn into villas that are really palaces – witness Fontainebleau and Chambord, and finally Versailles. The English monarchy, by contrast, did not have quite those resources, and the kings and queens were in the habit of descending on various nobles in their country seats – castles rather than palaces – for their country pleasures. Henry VIII, however, did build himself a palace-villa at Nonesuch in Surrey. Its name implied its unusual and ambitious character. When the king died, it was sold privately and frittered away; England could not yet afford such a royal villa and only a few drawings of it have survived. A century later, Anne of Denmark, James I's tall and clever queen, had Inigo Jones build her a house spanning the Deptford-Woolwich

road at Greenwich, still called the "Queen's House" (though she died before it was finished). That building marks the beginning of a new trend, since a curious association came about between the two oligarchic seafaring states, Venice and Britain. The splendid houses built in the previous century in the Po valley, particularly those of Palladio, became the model on which the English country gentleman extended, rebuilt, and even built anew his country house. It also, in the eighteenth century, became the center from which European agriculture was reformed and capitalized.

The English country house became the model for certain American landowners. But the ground on which American building took root was very different, particularly in the south, where the sun demanded more shelter than was ever needed in the cloud-capped British Isles. Yet there is a clear link between the Venetian houses of the Po valley, the English country house, and the American landowner's mansion. They were much farther from towns – American distances were completely unprecedented – and therefore not really villas in the ancient sense, even though their layout and accommodation often followed more or less the recipes of Columella.

In the twentieth century the villa has almost become the dominant house type. The way of life of the affluent, as it is shown in the cinema and in the soap opera, is the villa existence: the two-story house, the gardens and the farmland, the ubiquitous swimming pool, and always the implication of distance from the city of business and stress. At a lower income level, it is of course the model for the suburban house, particularly in North America. Will the villa survive into the era of the gated suburb? It looks like it, though it may be *otium* at too high a price.

Room of the Great Fresco,
detail of the Initiation into the
Dionysiac Mystery Rites

Villa of the Mysteries

Pompeii, Italy, 1st century AD

All Europe was excited by the rumors of the discovery of Pompeii and Herculaneum.
It started fitfully – a statue here, a tomb there, and private excavation before 1720.
Just before 1750, however, government-aided archaeologists almost immediately
uncovered "the house of the philosopher" at Herculaneum with its considerable
library, and many writings by a previously unknown Epicurean philosopher. From
then on excavations were more or less energetic. Herculaneum, under fifteen to
twenty feet of lava, proved more rewarding than Pompeii, which had been covered
by a relatively shallow and porous layer of ash, and what had stuck up above ground
had already been looted in antiquity.

Cubiculum 16,
detail of the wall painting in
the Second Style, c. 60 BC

The Neapolitans were secretive about the discoveries. The king had them published, slowly, in enormous folio volumes that he would give only to favored persons. But the news soon got out and the pilgrimages started. Goethe, on a visit to Naples in 1787, makes much of his joy at examining what was then very new and astounding. Until that time little was known about private houses. There were some fragments of course and in about 1500 the discovery of the baths of Titus, which were known as the *grotte* (so that their elaborate decorations came to be known as *grottesche),* started a craze in Rome that was fueled by Raphael's decorations in the Vatican palace. But it was not clear how all this might relate to the private house. Now in Pompeii and Herculaneum, complete cities, with ensembles of public and private spaces, were suddenly revealed.

The destruction of Pompeii by a great eruption of Vesuvius on August 24, AD 79, is described in Pliny the Younger's account of his uncle's death in a letter to Tacitus:

About one in the afternoon, my mother desired him to observe a cloud which appeared of a very unusual size and shape . . . he immediately arose and went out upon an eminence from whence he might more distinctly view this very uncommon appearance . . . it was found afterwards to ascend from mount Vesuvius . . . it appeared sometimes bright and sometimes dark and spotted, as it was either more or less impregnated with earth and cinders.[1]

Pliny the Elder then heroically went to the aid of a neighbor, Rectina, and to observe the extraordinary phenomenon and record it for posterity. He then realized his own danger. With an air of unconcern, he bathed and sat down cheerfully to eat, though not to sleep, but was eventually persuaded to leave the house with a pillow tied round his head with a napkin. It was too late, however, and on reaching the shore, they found that "the waves still ran extremely high and boisterous. There my uncle . . . was suffocated, as I conjecture, by some gross and noxious vapor, having always had weak lungs. . . ." Pliny relates his own

1. Pliny the Younger, *The Letters,* Book VI, Letter 16.

Room of the Great Fresco,
detail of the Initiation into the
Dionysiac Mystery Rites

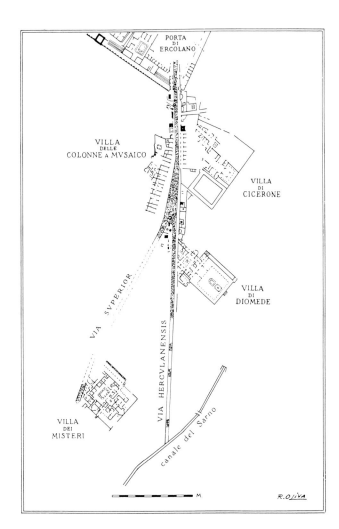

Plan of road into Pompeii lined with villas

escape with his mother in a subsequent letter and the desperate cries of the population lamenting their fate. Then there was silence as the whole town was enveloped by the ash.

After the first official publication of the finds, many unofficial ones followed. And further discoveries were made as more of the town was uncovered and as the surroundings began to be investigated. The Villa at Boscoreale was discovered about 1890, and its decorations moved to the Metropolitan Museum of Art in New York. However, in 1930, an even more sensational find was made not far from the Pompeii city gate. Raised on vaulted storage rooms was a villa surrounded by a peristyle, a portico on three sides of the house. It faces

southwest and gives a view of the sea. One of the rooms opening off the portico, the Room of the Great Fresco, is decorated with the painted scenes of a Dionysiac mystery rite, probably a form of initiation. Dionysiac mystery rites were forbidden several times in Rome, most severely in 185 BC, in Cato's lifetime, but the ban was defied in spite of bloody persecution. In any case, this room is too accessible and public to have been a "secret" chamber but the paintings are so vivid and brilliant that they have given the name to the villa.

Excavations are certainly not exhausted: an even more splendidly frescoed villa was uncovered a little farther away from the town in 1980, at a site that was named Oplontis. It is thought at one point to have been owned by Poppea Sabina, Nero's second wife.

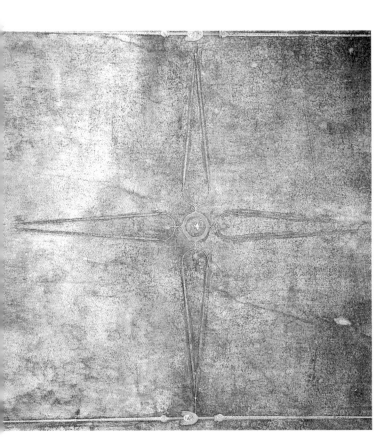

Cubiculum 16, detail

Cubiculum 16, detail of a dancing satyr

Atrium, view toward the peristyle

Following pages: Room of the Great Fresco, Initiation into the Dionysiac Mystery Rites

Hadrian's Villa

Tivoli, Italy, after AD 120

Born probably in Spain (his mother came from Cadiz), Hadrian was adopted by Trajan, whose great-niece he married, and whom he succeeded as emperor. He was one of the most literate and capable, as well as best-traveled, of all the emperors. His early familiarity with Greek and his affection for Greek ways earned him the nickname *Graeculus*. And he transformed Athens: his gate, his agora and library, the finishing of the huge temple of Olympic Zeus were undertaken when he was there and consecrated on another journey. He certainly visited Asia Minor, North Africa, Gaul, and the Germanic provinces. The decision to run a wall from the Tyne to the Solway against the Picts was made when he was in the north of England. His journey down the Nile and the death (perhaps by suicide or by murder) of his favorite, Antinous, whom he commemorated in a number of statues, are notorious.

Detail of the statue Tiber

Preceding pages: Canopus

Where and how he got his familiarity with architecture is not known; he was a great administrator and diplomat but the evidence of his direct involvement with the design of buildings has never been conclusive. The Pantheon in Rome, with its huge dome of poured concrete, is not only an extraordinary design but also a great feat of organization. The vast bulk of his mausoleum on the Tiber is now the Castel Sant'Angelo, and he was also responsible for the temple of Venus and Rome on the Roman Forum. There were almost certainly drawings by him (or by some anonymous draftsman) since he was in correspondence about them with Trajan's preferred architect, Apollodorus of Damascus (whose disrespectful comments on the imperial project led to his exile and perhaps to his death).

The Tiburtine villa may have been designed by the emperor himself about AD 120, probably as a model – or perhaps a summary – of the empire. It is just under twenty miles out of Rome. As it covered some eight square miles, it could hardly be considered a villa in the usual sense. It included any number of interrelated and very complex volumes, approached along directed vistas. There were different entrances for ambassadors, retainers, and the emperor himself. It had a Greek and a Latin theater, baths of varying complexity, barracks for soldiers, and lodgings for slaves, as well as numerous temples. The different parts carry references, which are not always clear now, and which the emperor never explained. A long pool, the *Canopus*, and its *serapeum* obviously suggest Egypt and, even more specifically, Alexandria. The Atheneum clearly refers to Athens, but so does the colonnaded space called

Service quarters

poikile after the stoa of the same name in that city, and this had the *ambulatio* on one side, a long wall, which was primarily intended to allow the emperor and his entourage to take walks in the shade. As the group of buildings was constructed over a long period of time and may have been added to haphazardly, the overall plan is difficult to read.

Of the theaters, the Greek one has survived in part: the seats (with the corridors beneath them) and proscenium are still very visible. The Latin theater, on the other hand, has been much restored. The east end of the *poikile* opens in a triclinium, a banqueting hall, which connects to a "sporting" complex with a swimming pool and a stadium. The other side of the *poikile* adjoins a niched hall, which in turn leads into a mysterious circular fountain building, sometimes called *Naumachia*, sometimes *Nymphaeum*,

but whose purpose has never been explicit. Beyond is the library court, which has both a Latin and a Greek library, as well as guest rooms, and further, the emperor's own quarters and the complex *Piazza d'Oro*, which seems to have been a solemn reception space – or perhaps even a sanctuary.

Beyond the *Piazza d'Oro* lie two bath buildings, now known as the "large" and the "small," though they are similar in size. Any larger villa would have had such baths, and in cities they become vast, monumental complexes – on which nineteenth-century railway buildings were based. Of course they were not meant for washing, but were luxurious predecessors of the Turkish bath. A colonnaded room would contain a *baptisterium*, or cold-water basin, at the center for a preliminary wash in the open, linked to the *Apodyterium* or *Spolatorium,* the dressing room. The bather would then proceed through chambers with controlled temperatures: from the *Frigidarium* (for cold bathing under cover) to the *Tepidarium* with swimming pools and meeting rooms. He or she then reached the usually circular *Caldarium* or *Sudatorium* (a type of steam bath for which instructions are carefully given by Vitruvius) and then might have a scented-oil massage in the *Unctorium*. There were summer and winter bathing areas, and, as in Hadrian's, many of them included *Scholae*, gathering places for discussions and readings. In Republican times there might be she and he baths, but later the separation was effected by different bathing times for men and women, though some of them seemed to have been unisex with discussions in undress, though this practice was frowned on and abolished by Hadrian himself.

Plan of the villa complex

private suite (libraries)

maritime theater

Poikile

triclinium

stadium

Piazza d'Oro

Small Baths

vestibule

Large Baths

N

0   250m
0   500ft

Canopus

Piazza d'Oro

Academy

Large Baths

The Alhambra

Granada, Spain, 13th–14th centuries

Alhambra is a corruption of the Arab name "the Red Citadel," *El-Qal'at el'hamra,* awarded either because of the color of the sun-dried bricks of which the outer walls of the fortress in Granada are built, or more graphically, because of the red flares that were lit as workers labored through the nights to complete the building. The Alhambra was constructed in the reign of Mohammed Ibn al-Ahmar, the founder of the Nasrid Sultanate that lasted until its expulsion from the last Moorish kingdom in 1492. The sultans were, on the whole, cultivated and liberal, so that the Nasrid court attracted many moslem scholars, as well as architects, painters, and sculptors, though none left their name on any of the artworks that survive.

Courtyard of the Lions, detail of a column

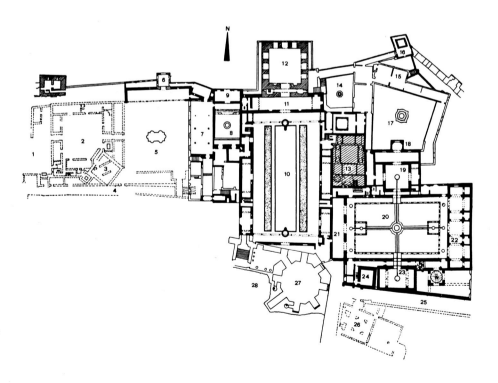

1. Entrance plaza
2. Court of the Madrassah of the Princes
3. Mosque ruins
4. Street
5. Court of Machuca
6. Tower of Machuca
7. Mexuar
8. Courtyard of the Golden Room
9. Golden Room
10. Courtyard of the Myrtles
11. Barca Gallery
12. Tower of the Comares and Hall of Ambassadors
13. Comares Baths

14. Court of the Iron Gate
15. Charles V's Apartments
16. Peinador Tower
17. Court of Daraxa
18. Mirador of Daraxa
19. Hall of the Two Sisters
20. Courtyard of the Lions
21. Mucarnos Gallery
22. Hall of the Kings
23. Hall of the Abencerrajes
24. Cistern
25. Fosse (moat)
26. Rauda or Muslim Cemetery
27. Crypt of Charles V's Palace
28. Palace of Charles V

Granada was an Iberian, then a Roman, and finally a Vandal town before it was taken by the Caliphs of Cordoba in the eighth century. The hill, which dominates the town but offers, on a clear day, a breathtaking view of the Sierra Nevada, was certainly fortified early on. The present fortress was begun by al-Ahmar; he also took about a tenth of the area for a single-story palace articulated by courtyards within, many fountains and narrow water-channels tattooing the smooth stone floors. The whole complex, a rectangular court with surrounding chambers, with gardens and the dependent villa called Generalife (Jennat al-Arif, the architect's garden), covers some thirty-five acres. All the exteriors are plain, almost severe, while the magnificent, elaborately pat-terned interiors – the walls seem almost woven and are finely carved, painted, and gilt – were completed under Jusef I, who died in 1354. The colors were initially bright and are now much faded, though the dados and lower walls that were faced with enameled tiles have retained their sparkle.

The Catholic kings, Ferdinand and Isabella, having expelled Boabil, the last Nasrid, cared nothing for the palace and its decorations. Rooms were subdivided, decorations white-washed or defaced, furniture wrecked or carted away. Their descendant, Charles V (r. 1516–56), who did appreciate the splendid Mesquita in Cordoba, had an apartment made for his own use in the Alhambra and started the huge square palace on the site of the destroyed win-ter quarters, which blocks the Courtyard of

Gilded cupola

Courtyard of the Myrtles

the Myrtles and seemed an "arrogant intrusion" to Washington Irving. Under Philip V (r. 1700–46) some rooms were "modernized." In 1812 the building was attacked by the French and two of the towers blown up, and in 1821 it was shaken by an earthquake, though the balance of the structure escaped further degradation. Some of the roses and myrtles in the gardens were replaced by English elms imported by the Duke of Wellington. From about 1830 the Alhambra has been cared for respectfully and lovingly by three generations of architects from one family, the Contreras. Its history is best summed up by Washington Irving:

To believe that so much has survived the wear and tear of centuries, the shock of earthquakes, the violence of war and the quiet, though no less baneful, pilferings of the tasteful traveler: it is almost sufficient to excuse the popular tradition, that the whole is protected by magic charm.[1]

1. Geoffrey Crayon Gent, *The Alhambra or the New Sketch Book* (Paris, 1834), pp. 2ff.

Wall detail

Detail of a mosaic

Entrance facade and fountain

Bathroom

Wood cupola

Bathroom

Girolamo Genga Villa Imperiale Albani

Pesaro, Italy, c.1530

Pesaro in the Marches, on the Adriatic, is overshadowed by the small but splendid inland town of Urbino, where the *condottiere* Federico da Montefeltre held one of the most brilliant courts of the Renaissance. It was then sold to Alessandro, brother of Francesco Sforza, duke of Milan, and in 1452, when the emperor Frederic III passed through the town having been crowned by the pope, Alessandro entertained him lavishly and invited him to lay the foundation stone of a new palace-villa (hence to be called Imperiale) on Monte Accio, which overlooks the town and owes its name to Lucius Accius, a grammarian and tragic poet who was more or less contemporary with Varro. Lucius Accius was supposed to have been born and buried on this spot (though the dramatic genius now associated with Pesaro is its much more recent native son, Gioacchino Rossini), which was celebrated both because of its splendid views and its beneficent climate.

View from the southeast

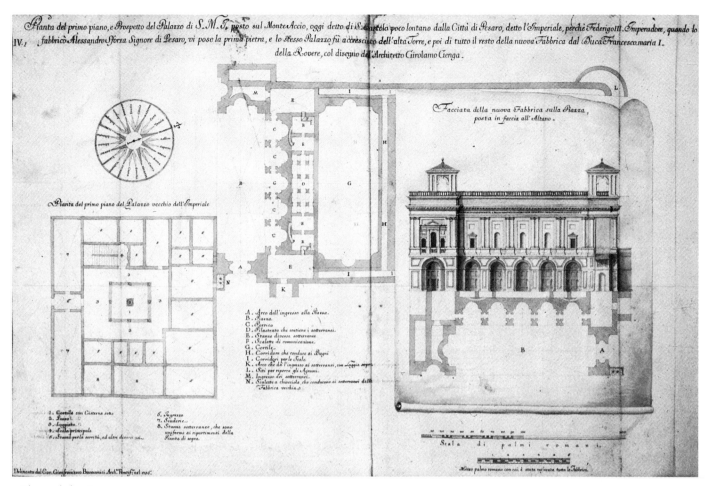

Plan and elevation

Lorenzo Lorana, the original (and probably Dalmatian) architect of the palace at Urbino, also designed Alessandro Sforza's town palace; he and the great Sienese architect Francesco di Giorgio had worked in the small duchy. (Its most famous architect was in fact Donato Bramante, active in Milan after 1480 and chief papal architect since about 1500; his nephew, Raphael, became even more famous. Neither of them worked in their hometown after they left for Rome.) Alessandro first employed Lorana on the villa. On his death Pesaro reverted to the Montefeltre dukes of Urbino, and the della Roveres (the family of Pope Julius II) became the heirs of the extinct Montefeltre.

Francesco Maria della Rovere and his wife, Leonora Gonzaga, employed Girolamo Genga as a painter and theatrical decorator as well as architect. Genga (1476–1551) was a native of Urbino who had already acquired a great reputation as the pupil and then assistant of Luca Signorelli. He went on to work with Pietro Perugino, where Raphael was also a pupil. Because of his growing reputation, Francesco Maria then convinced him to come home. Besides his professional skills, which included festival and theatrical decorations, he had the reputation of a great charmer and good companion as well as an accomplished musician; in fact no one seems to have had a bad word to say about him.

Duchess Leonora was determined to finish the Villa Imperiale in emulation of the splendid Villa Madama, which Raphael was building on the Monte Mario overlooking Rome, and to

Following pages: Portico leading to the secret garden

commemorate her husband's return from his stint as commander of the Venetian armies and had rooms decorated with their joint initials. Genga's contribution lay not only in the design of the new buildings (one of which, a 120-foot tower with an internal wooden staircase, was much admired for its ingenuity, though it has not survived) but also in the selection of the painters to decorate the rooms. They included Raffaello dal Colle and the young Bronzino, as well as the Dossi brothers, Dosso and Battista (whose paintings unfortunately proved unacceptable and were replaced).

When the della Rovere dukes died out in their turn, the villa passed to the Florentine Medici, who had no real interest in it. In the mid-eighteenth century it was adapted to serve as temporary lodgings for the Jesuits expelled from Spain and Portugal, and it then passed to the Albani, the family of Clement XI, who was from Urbino and served as pope between 1730 and 1740. It was partially restored by them about a hundred years ago. There has not been a serious study of it for nearly a century.

The buildings, which for several generations were the background of an extraordinary court, are being restored after nearly three centuries of neglect. They have a brilliant internal arrangement of sunken courtyards and a rather solemn, antique articulation, and the play between the deep recessions at ground level and the planar manner of the *piano nobile* suggests that Genga was inspired by Bramante's inventive treatment of the long walls in the great courtyard of the Vatican Belvedere, but wanted to push the possibilities of modeling such a surface more dramatically.

Genga and Francesco Menzocchi da Forlì, detail of the painted ceiling in the Pope Clement XI Hall decorated with the initials of the duke and duchess

Hall of the Oath

Hall of the Calumny, the allegory of Charity

The Room of the Caryatids, female figures

Following pages: Hall of the Calumny, mythical scene of the apotheosis of Francesco Maria I della Rovere

Giacomo da Vignola # Villa Lante

Bagnaia, Italy, 1556–80

Viterbo was a neighboring diocese of the pope's, and the bishop was often a cardinal. In around 1200 the city of Viterbo gave the bishop the village of Bagnaia, and he would often use it as a hunting park and summer residence. When a bishop would try to leave the property to his family, his successors would always claim it back. The great days of Bagnaia began when Raffaele Riario, nephew of Sixtus IV, built the hunting lodge that still stands in the park, and it was he who started the custom of bishops spending summers there. In 1532 Cardinal Niccolo Ridolfi – whose uncle was the Medici Leo X – got use of the local water and built an aqueduct to the site. Gian Francesco Gambara, one of those who insisted on getting the park back for his see (which he held for more than twenty years), started work on the villa and the gardens as soon as he got possession of them, in 1556.

No written documents or drawings exist to prove authorship, but an old tradition, as well as probability, attributes the design to Giacomo Barozzi da Vignola (1507–73), the same architect who had worked with Giacomo della Porta at St. Peter's, and who had designed the vast castle-palace-villa at Caprarola, nearby, for the Farnese family.

Much must already have been done by 1580, when the austere Cardinal Charles Borromeo (canonized soon after his death), returning to his see, Milan, passed through Bagnaia; he apparently told Gambara that he would have done better giving his money away to the poor than spending it on such flummery. Work stopped, and money went to a hospital. Montaigne, who visited it a year later, was not as scandalized, and seems to have been shown around by a "Monsieur Thomas" (perhaps the head gardener) in the cardinal's absence. Work, particularly on the frescoes and the fountains, was then continued under another cardinal-bishop, Alessandro Peretti, who, like his uncle Sixtus V, took the title Montalto from their native village.

Entry is through a large, square, formal garden, all of whose elaborately clipped beds are also square. The garden has been restored in recent times to its early-eighteenth-century form. At the center is a pool, with a stone, boat-shaped fountain in each quarter, while the central circular pool is surmounted by four "moors," each of whom carries a pear (a punning allusion to the family name, Peretti); all unite to hold high the mountain of the family arms, Montalto, which replaces the pyramid that had been put there in Cardinal Gambara's time.

On either side of the ramped slope, which takes the visitor up to the next level, stand the two identical square *palazzine,* Montalto and Gambara. They are charming rather than grand: a basement pierced by three arches makes agreeable *loggie* overlooking the lower garden, while the *piano nobile* is pilastered; the pyramidal roof has a crowning square belvedere as a lantern. At the high point of the gardens is the mossy and weedy fountain called "The Flood," which feeds all the waterworks at Bagnaia. On either side are smaller twin pavilions decorated with Cardinal Gambara's crest (another pun, on *Gambero*), the crayfish. The downward water course is broken by many fountains, most conspicuously by the "water chain," an elaborately carved cascade (of a kind much loved by gardeners in the seventeenth century). Between the two principal *palazzine,* the water is taken in a runnel through a long stone bench, known as the "Cardinal's Table," which was in fact used for open-air banquets.

The gardens and the painted interiors are the glories of the Villa Lante. The first *palazzina,* built by Riario, has smaller rooms, painted by local artists, but the second one, added by Peretti, has a grand salon painted by Cavalier d'Arpino. The best known of the painters who worked there was Agostino Tassi (now chiefly remembered as having been tried for raping another pupil, Artemisia Gentileschi), though his fame is also due to the fact that he was the teacher of the great French landscape painter Claude, who worked as an assistant at Bagnaia. Many others were involved, working for the two cardinals: Raffaellino da Reggio, Antonio Tempesta, and perhaps the best of them all, Artemisia's father, Orazio Gentileschi.

Raffaellino da Reggio and assistants, a seventeenth-century fresco with a view of the villa, in the loggia of the Palazzina Gambara

Following pages: View of the upper garden with the Fountain of the Moors

*The "water chain," with a series of
waterfalls in the foreground, the
Fountain of the Cardinal's Table,
and the Fountain of the Moors*

*The Fountain of the Lights, with the
Fountain of the Giants, representing
the Tiber and Arno rivers, in the
background*

The small grotto of Neptune

*The Fountain of Pegasus with
Palazzina Gambara on the right*

Pirro Ligorio Casino of Pius IV

Rome, Italy, c. 1559

Of a noble Neapolitan family, Pirro Ligorio (1513–1583) came to Rome in 1534, just out of his teens. He was making a living as a fresco-facade painter, in a manner that an older master, Perino del Vaga, had perfected, but he soon became known as an assiduous antiquarian. He then began working on a vast compendium of Roman antiquities, of which two somewhat different manuscript versions exist. Although it became clear (mostly after his death) that Ligorio's excavation reports were heavily doctored, his surveys completed by speculative reconstructions, and his antique coins often invented, in spite of his aggression and intolerance, his reputation stood high in his lifetime.

*Head of the Medusa, detail
of the loggia facade*

Cardinal Ippolito II d'Este (son of Lucrezia Borgia), the great magnifico and collector of the papal court, appointed Ligorio antiquarian when he became governor of Tivoli in 1550, and charged him with excavating Hadrian's villa nearby – for collectibles, regrettably. The commission did, however, allow him to establish the first complete plan of the villa, on which he continued to work even after he had been forced out of Rome. He was then asked to arrange the monastic buildings Ippolito had been given as governor, and transformed them into a palace with famous gardens whose cascades were musically commemorated by Franz Liszt in *Jeux d'Eaux à la Villa d'Este*. In 1558 Ligorio entered the service of his countryman, Pope Paul IV (Carafa, who had been elected in 1555 at age seventy-nine and whose tomb Ligorio was to design). He was subsequently involved in work on St. Peter's with Michelangelo, and succeeded him jointly with Vignola, though jealousy and unwarranted accusations of malpractice on the part of the architect and sculptor Giacomo della Porta led to his imprisonment for several months in 1565. When the rather dour Paul IV died in 1559, Ligorio was employed by the more generous and relaxed next pope, Pius IV (of the Milanese branch of the Medici), to complete and to decorate the pope's *casino*. It was recognized as the most perfect retreat for a sunny afternoon (according to Jacob Burckhardt in his *Cicerone*). It was also the time of the last sessions of the Council of Trent, which was finally closed in 1564, and the rather irenic Pius was, until the end, hopeful of a rapprochement with at least some Protestants.

Detail of the sculpture on the casino facade

A. Decorative two-story hall
B. First floor: vestibule with polychrome
   marble floor; second floor: gallery
C. First floor: papal retreat and chapel;
   second floor: two-story tower

1. Loggia
2. Oval courtyard
3. Casino entrance portico

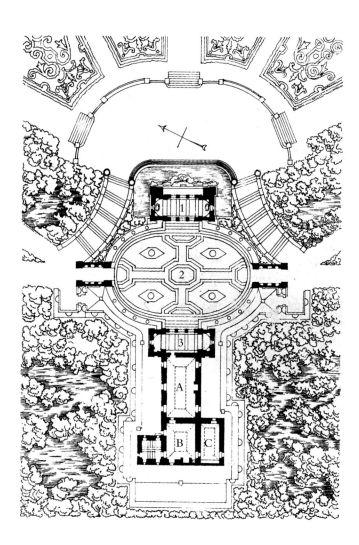

Death of Adonis, *fresco on the*
loggia vault by Federico Zuccaro

Preceding pages: The loggia facade

The casino, which had the pope's enthusiastic and even obsessive attention, is sited on a slope; the two buildings that compose it – the casino proper and the loggia – are separated by an oval courtyard, and the grouping ends in a sculptural fountain (which has unfortunately been badly mauled). The complex program of richly molded neo-pagan relief decorations and explicitly Christian frescoes provides a discreet dialectic between the types of ancient myth and of those offered by scripture, and is in some sense a commentary on papal hopes. Ligorio seems to have designed all the reliefs and inscriptions himself, but the frescoes are the work of a number of different painters, notably Federico Barocci and Federico Zuccaro, who were more highly esteemed at the time than they are now.

Though set within the Vatican gardens, visible from the palace windows and almost in the shadow of St. Peter's, the casino was intended as a place of private retreat and seclusion for successive popes, though today it has passed into the possession of the Pontificia Accademia delle Scienze.

Entrance portico of the casino.
The Song of Circe is by artists
in the circle of Federico Zuccaro

Entrance portico of the casino

Detail of one of the two exedrae in
the entrance portico of the casino

Following pages: Facade of the
loggia facing the garden

Andrea Palladio # Villa Rotonda

Vicenza, Italy, 1560s

Of all Palladio's villas, this is the one most closely identified with his name and manner, as well as the most imitated. It is also nearest to Vicenza, the town in which he spent most of his life. Andrea Palladio was born in Padua in 1508; little is known about his background, except that his family seems to have been involved in boats, hence the name "della Gondola," by which he was sometimes known. "Palladius" was a nickname given him by his first patron, the noble diplomat, antiquarian, and poet Gian Giorgio Trissino. He was certainly using the name "Andrea Palladio" by about 1540.

He came of age at a time of Venetian expansion and increased self-confidence, when two other city-states, Verona and Padua (and Vicenza with them), had been absorbed into the Republic. It led to a reduction in petty warfare, so that the unfortified country residence became particularly attractive to the Venetian gentry. This was important, as Venice was losing its hold on sea trade, which was being eroded by the new transatlantic navigation as well as the trade around the Cape of Good Hope. Mainland estates were therefore essential in providing the leading Venetian families with the income that assured their status in town. The villa-type invented by Palladio was a stroke of genius and assured his local, and later his international, fame. His association with another great Venetian figure, Daniele Barbaro, patriarch of Aquilea and the most important churchman-scholar in Venice, ensured his position as the most prestigious architect of the Republic; he designed the two largest and most prominent churches built in Venice in his time, both of them domed: San Giorgio and the Redentore. He was also a prolific author, and his treatise on architecture, *Quattro libri dell'architettura*, became one of the most popular books on architecture in Europe and later in America. Palladio's manner of building was therefore adopted eagerly by his local patrons, and because of the close relation between Stuart Britain and the Venetian Republic, it also became an ideal in the Britain of James I and Charles I. Inigo Jones, the court architect of the two kings, bought a copy of Palladio's *Quattro libri* on his travels, which he annotated and used.

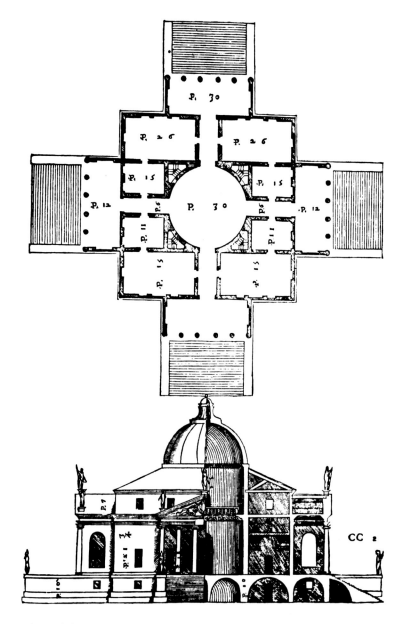

Plan and elevation

The Villa Rotonda (also called Capra after its later owners; the Valmarana family acquired and restored it in the twentieth century) was designed and built quickly, probably between 1566 and 1569, for Monsignor Paolo Almerico, a Vicentine who had held office at the court of popes Pius IV and V, and who was also very rich. The villa is square in plan, and its corners face the main compass points, so that none of the Ionic porticoes on each of its four sides is ever without some sunlight. There is a dome over the central cylindrical room (hence the name *Rotonda*). Almerico had given some spectacular parties and receptions, probably on the future site of the villa, so that it acquired the reputation of being merely a belvedere from which to watch firework displays. This would explain why, unlike Palladio's other villas, it was planned without the *barchesse*, the usual farm outbuildings, though they were added later by the subsequent owners who settled down to a more commonplace existence. Whether intended as a permanent home for Almerico or as a belvedere, the Rotonda is unique among Palladio's houses in its symmetry about two axes; the dome gives it a certain solemnity.

Some scholars have maintained that the villa was completed after 1600, following Palladio's death in 1580, by Vincenzo Scamozzi, his most learned and prolific disciple, who certainly worked on the building. The stuccos and the painted decorations, however, took another

century to complete. The statues on the exterior were done by different sculptors, and a number of painters worked on the interiors both for Almerico and for the Capras. Most of the rooms have elaborately painted allegorical ceilings, though authorities do not agree upon attributions: Bernardino India and Alessandro Canera (a Veronese painter, and a colleague of the great and famous Paolo Calliari, called Veronese) certainly made contributions; Giovanni Caroto is named in connection with other houses by Palladio, who also knew the two Maganzas, father Giambattista and son Alessandro, who worked in the Rotonda. Throughout the house these paintings are framed by splendid stuccoed ribs very much in harmony with Palladio's manner. The central spaces of the villa, however, were painted between 1690 and 1710 by Louis Dorigny, whose elaborate and forced perspectives introduced a new and somewhat jarring note into the interior.

The obsessive symmetry of the villa fascinated later architects who became familiar with depictions in engravings rather than the actual building. Scamozzi was much influenced by the Rotonda, particularly in his design for the Rocca Pisana in Lonigo. Through Palladio's treatise as well as Scamozzi's, the building became much admired and imitated, as by Lord Burlington at Chiswick House and Thomas Jefferson at his home, Monticello.

Central hall with frescoes by Alessandro Maganza, framed by stucchi attributed to Agostini Rubini. The decorative program extends from the entrance level up to the top of the dome

Central hall, the dome

Central hall, with frescoes by
Louis Dorigny

Central hall, view from the opposite end

Giacomo della Porta # Villa Aldobrandini

Frascati, Italy, 1598–1603

Frascati is about five miles closer to Rome than Tivoli, but farther south. It lies on the slope of the Alban Hills, and looks north toward Rome, across the Campagna. It is one of the Castelli Romani – a group of small towns where the popes and the great Roman families maintained country retreats. There was probably an imperial villa here at the time of Domitian, but nothing is left of it.

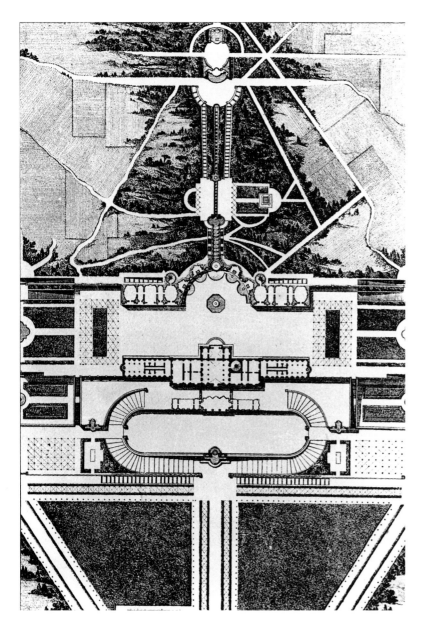

Plan of the villa and surrounding gardens

In the sixteenth century the papacy acquired a splendid battery of villas built by the Roman nobility. Cardinal Aldobrandini, one of the three cardinal-nephews of Clement VIII (r. 1592–1605, and "an unashamed nepotist," as one historian called him), was urged by his uncle, an old man, to build the villa while he was still alive. The cardinal wanted to rebuild the older house on the site, but Giacomo della Porta (1533–1602), one of the architects of St. Peter's whom he engaged (and whose last project it was), convinced him to pull it down and start anew. He did not live to finish it, but work was carried on by Carlo Maderno (who is chiefly remembered today for having extended Michelangelo's dome at St. Peter's) and his successor at the Vatican, Domenico Fontana, with his familiars.

The villa is often called a palace, and it is grand enough for that label. The site is an even incline and looks down over the Campagna toward Rome. The entrance facade is rather severe and is approached over an oval, stepped terrace. The garden facade, however, is complex and playful. As on the front, the central pavilion towers above the building and is pedimented, while the lower wings, articulated by slightly projecting rustication, are crowned by the end of an outsize broken pediment, as if they were fragments of a vast palace that had sunk into the ground but had once been covered by a huge roof. The central pavilion, whose much smaller pediment slopes a little more gently, can be "read" as if it were a newer and later – but harmonious – addition.

Preceding pages: Entrance facade

In front of the villa is yet another terrace (closed by formal gardens and woods to either side), which opens in a great hemicycle, called "the water theater." Through its central arch one can see the cascade, which feeds the fountains in the two niches on either side and they shelter statues of various mythological figures. The hemicycle extends on one side into a pavilion containing a water organ, a smaller version of the curious, gurgly musical instrument that Pirro Ligorio had installed at the

Villa d'Este and that Liszt celebrated, while the other side ends in an elaborately frescoed chapel dedicated to St. Sebastian, patron of the Aldobrandini. Unfortunately, the water-damaged frescoes had to be moved inside the main building. In the Room of Apollo, Domenichino painted some ten frescoes, which also suffered from water damage. Aldobrandini sold them to a restorer, and they eventually found a home at the National Gallery in London.

Following pages: Terrace between the garden facade and the water theater. The minaret is a kitchen chimney

Facade and side view

As for the cascade, it runs in an ornate, stepped bed, which conceals a number of piped water outlets; on either side of it are stairways. At the turning of a key – some of them are in the pavilion, others concealed along the stairs – these outlets can be activated to surprise and to drench the innocent passerby: a truly cardinalitial practical joke, some say. The stairways are crowned by two mosaiced spiral columns, which are also fountain-cascades and are the most prominent relics of the elaborate sculpture garden that was once the privileged promenade of the villa's inhabitants.

The central archway of the water theater is crowned by a small fountain that springs from a sculptured Aldobrandini star, the family's heraldic emblem. But the clan did not endure beyond 1680, and the villa was inherited by their relations by marriage, the Pamphilii, who were responsible for much of the splendid interior painting and decoration, including the seventeenth-century Leather Room, so called because the colorful and highly detailed decoration of *putti,* flowers, and fruit is tooled and stamped in the leather covering of its walls. The villa then passed to another great Roman family, the Borghese, whose late-nineteenth-century scion revived the Aldobrandini name on inheriting their possessions.

Detail of the Leather Room

Entrance hall, Cardinal Aldobrandini's name and title are inscribed over the fireplace

The Leather Room

The Chinese Room, named
after its nineteenth-century
Chinese wallpaper

The Room of Apollo, vault painted by
Tommaso and Domenico Passignano

Preceding pages: The water theater,
designed by Carlo Maderno and
engineered by Giovanni Fontana

The Room of Apollo, illusionistic
bower, detail of the painted vault

The Room of Apollo, detail of the wall

The Room of Apollo, with mosaic floor

Ange-Jacques Gabriel # Petit Trianon

Versailles, France, 1761–67

Posterity has been unkind to the Marquise de Pompadour, labeling her a *rococotte*, yet there was nothing of the cocotte about the rather straitlaced and literary lady. She was both charming and amusing to be sure, but definitely a bluestocking, even if she was the reigning mistress of the anything but virtuous Louis XV. She was also a declared enemy of the flighty and capricious style that we call rococo. Her brother, the Marquis de Marigny, who became the dispenser of French royal building patronage, had very much the same vices, and his favorite architect, who was also a personal friend, Jacques-Germain Soufflot, designed the building in Paris that became the manifesto of the new, sober neoclassical manner, the church of Ste. Geneviève, which has become known as the Panthéon.

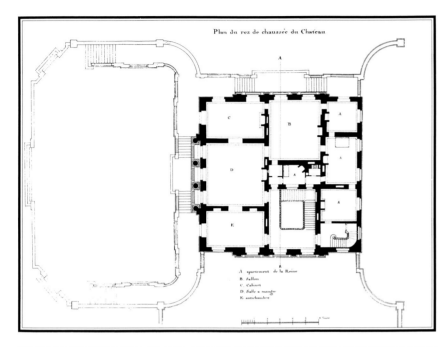

Plan du rez de chaussée du Château

A apartement de la Reine
B Sallon
C Cabinet
D Salle à manger
E antichambre

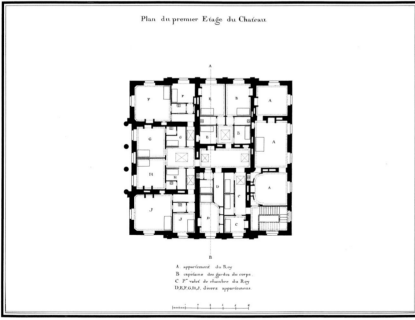

Plan du premier Etage du Château

A appartement du Roy
B capitaine des gardes du corps
C Pʳ valet de chambre du Roy
D,E,F,G,H,J, divers appartemens

Plans of the first and second floors

At the vast royal palace, Versailles, which had started its career as a hunting lodge for Louis XIII and became the main royal residence for Louis XIV, Marigny had exerted some control over the royal building budget. Many architects had worked there, but the main figures trusted by Louis XIV were the Mansarts – uncle François and nephew Jules-Hardouin. Inside the park Jules-Hardouin had already designed for Louis XIV a retreat from the *negotium* of the court, where the elaborate ceremonial could be dropped and the king could relax among his favorites. This retreat was called the Grand Trianon.

Ange-Jacques Gabriel (1698–1782) was born into a family of architects, many of them connected to the court. His father, Jacques, bought (as was usual at the time) his position as *Contrôleur Général des Bâtiments du Roi* from the widow of a Mansart cousin and bequeathed it to Ange-Jacques, who was also to be active at Versailles. It was his good fortune to find a particularly enlightened patron in Louis XV. Ange-Jacques became *Premier Architecte* in 1742 and thereafter was responsible for designing, or at least administering, most royal – and therefore state – building work, the various châteaux of the king (Choisy, Fontainebleau, Compiègne, La Muette), and much rebuilding in Paris and in provincial cities. The Place Louis XV (now de la Concorde) is in outline as he designed it; so is his other major project in Paris, the Ecole Militaire of 1751 on the left bank.

West facade

At Versailles, the Opéra in the main palace was Gabriel's first major building. He then took over a *ménagerie,* a small animal-breeding station that adjoined a botanic garden just beyond the Trianon, where coffee and pineapple were grown. Near the garden, the king, who had a lively interest in natural history, had another private two-story palace built by Gabriel: a *petit château* – the Petit Trianon. It was also intended as a retreat for the king and Mme de Pompadour, who supervised the decorations and even presented two fireplaces from her Parisian house (now the Palais de l'Elysée, the residence of the French president) for its completion. Unfortunately, it was not ready until 1767, three years after she died, though Louis XV ordered that her recommendations be followed everywhere. The next king, the unfortunate Louis XVI, made a present of the Petit Trianon to his rather indiscreet consort, Marie Antoinette. She redecorated some of the interiors in a more brittle version of the same manner as had pleased Mme de Pompadour, though the plan and the volumes of Gabriel's very ingenious scheme have remained.

Because of the gentle slope of the site, the square building is not identical on four sides and has only two stories: a tall *piano nobile* on the ground floor and a much squatter attic over it. They are unified by four Corinthian columns, which are detached columns on the garden facade, but are flattened into pilasters on two other sides. The cornice of the columns and the balustrade hide the slopes of the roof, so that the facade appears to be an articulated rectangle – its height is half its length. The whole plan is a single square, modulated very subtly. The ground floor was intended for entertaining – more or less privately – even if the mechanical tables, which could be entirely set with food in the kitchen and hoisted to the dining room (thus excluding servants from royal intimacies), were not executed. Of the original interiors, probably the most splendid relic is the square staircase, its wrought-iron balustrade designed (it is said) by the king himself. The attic, originally intended for Louis XV's scientific pursuits as well as a private apartment, was used exclusively by Marie Antoinette. The queen also had her own architect, Robert Mique, build her a private opera house on the grounds; it remains intact – with an elaborate stage whose machinery is in working order.

The grounds were radically changed. Mme de Pompadour's formal, scientifically planned garden was transformed by Marie Antoinette into a then fashionable landscaped English park; the animal-breeding station was transformed into a picturesque cottage adjoined by a toy dairy, where the queen would play at milkmaids with her companions.

North facade, seen through the gate
outside the lower garden entrance

Robert Adam Syon House

Middlesex, England, 1762–63

The Percys of Northumberland were a notch above other dukes – even if the line of succession was not always straightforward. Almost sovereign in their county on the Scottish borders, they kept the last court to have a liveried, uniformed jester at Alnwick Castle. Their town palace, Northumberland House, was pulled down to give way to Northumberland Avenue and the lines to Charing Cross station in 1874. Syon was their London villa.

Like the houses of many British noblemen, Syon had been a convent – an early fifteenth-century nunnery of the Bridgetines, first established by Henry V. James I gave the ruined convent to the then earl in about 1620, but it had never been properly adapted. About 1760 the duke decided to transform it, though only three sides of the ambitious scheme were carried out. The circular center court and the monumental staircase that appear on the project were never begun.

As at Alnwick and Northumberland House, the Northumberlands used Robert Adam (1728–92) as their architect at Syon. The Adam office was a family affair. William, its founder, was himself the son of a successful builder and contractor; he had four sons and six daughters. Two of the girls helped run the London practice, while two others married "well" inasmuch as these connections were later to prove very useful to their brothers. Three sons became architects: John was the eldest and the only one who worked in Scotland; James and Robert (who was the most energetic and enterprising of the brood) moved to London.

William Adam operated very successfully in Scotland. This meant that Robert felt sufficiently secure and confident about his future prospects to set out in 1754 on his Grand Tour, which would last some four years. He spent most of it in Rome – setting up as a milord

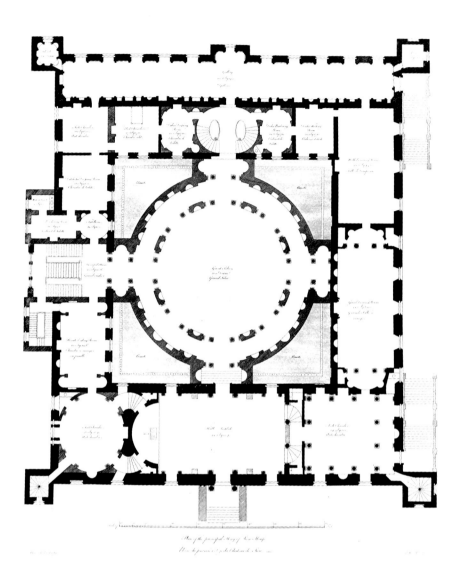

Ground-floor plan

The Great Hall, with antique statues and busts at either end of the hall, and statues of the Dying Gaul and the Apollo Belvedere within the apses

Ceiling of the Entrance Hall, with stucco by the Joseph Rose workshop

(which allowed him to make very useful contacts) rather than as a student. When he returned in 1758 he started a London branch of the practice. He had brought two draftsmen back with him from Rome, as well as a great quantity of drawings and antiquities, and was determined to introduce the new "Grand Style" into Britain. In 1764 one step was accomplished: the publication of the survey (done mostly by one of those draftsmen, a Frenchman, Charles-Louis Clérisseau) of the palace of the emperor Diocletian at Split, in Dalmatia.

At Syon, Robert showed himself master of the new style, as well as a most ingenious planner in adapting the graceless shapes of the old building to new spatial and decorative demands. The exterior was sheathed in Bath stone about 1825, and new windows with the thin glazing bars the Adams preferred were substituted for the older coarse ones. Robert's energy, however, was reserved for the interior. Since the Grand Hall was a half level below the *piano nobile*, he made it virtually a double cube, its geometry underlined by the diagonal coffering of the ceiling and the black-and-white marble patterning of the floor. Its order is Doric and its ornaments white and gray, typical of the entries of Adam houses. Two curved stairways lead to an anteroom, brightly colored and gilt, its awkward shape tidied up into a square by the Ionic columnar screen of *verde antico* marble; the floor is highly polished scagliola, a combination of marble, fixing, and coloring materials. Some left-over space is transformed into a

Anteroom

vestibule, with one end closed off for the newly invented water closet. Turning from the anteroom one passes two oblong rooms: the first has screened apses; the second is a plain rectangle, which had been hung with red damask, its coffered ceiling painted by Angelika Kauffman, which in turn admits one into an excessively long gallery, its awkward shape mitigated and sweetened by a complex design that consists of rhythmically varied pilasters on the walls and a network of ribs on the ceiling that picks up these articulations and plays on them diagonally. This pattern is further punctuated by medallions of the illustrious Percys by various hands. The ceiling ornamentation is echoed in a carpet that follows the Adam designs.

Anteroom, with a gilt copy of a statue of the Medici faun supplied by John Cheere positioned on top of an Ionic column

Joseph Rose, cherub against a gilded panel based on the Trophy of Marius *on the Capitol*

Following pages: Anteroom, detail of an Ionic column

Dining room, detail of a Corinthian column

Dining room, with alcove statues by sculptors including Joseph Wilton and Bartolomeo Cavaceppi. Grisaille paintings by Andrea Casali

Long Gallery, a section of the
paneled ceiling. The paintings are
attributed to Francesco Zuccarelli

Preceding pages: Anteroom,
chimney piece marble relief by
Thomas or Benjamin Carter

The Long Gallery is punctuated by a
series of bookshelves and alcoves. The
carpet, made in 1967, incorporates the
original 1765 design by Angelo Pergolesi

Following pages: West facade

Thomas Jefferson # Monticello

Charlottesville, Virginia, 1771–82

Whatever the truth of Thomas Jefferson's (1743–1826) family life, the third president of the United States was a man of vast intellect, outstanding ability, and lasting influence. Elected to the first Virginia convention in 1774 (even if he could not attend it), he proposed resolutions for the Continental Congress in Philadelphia that were immediately published in a pamphlet entitled *A Summary View of the Rights of America*, which was widely circulated on both sides of the Atlantic; it made him one of the leaders of the Revolution. Revised portions of his text were later incorporated into the Declaration of Independence.

Jefferson lived in France as minister at a crucial time in that country's history, between 1784 and 1789, and this experience enhanced his belief in limited central government and individual responsibility. When he retired from the presidency to his estates in Virginia, following two terms between 1801 and 1809, he had spent over forty years in public service, and he continued to be consulted by his immediate successors, James Madison and James Monroe, to the end of his life.

The son of a civil engineer, Jefferson seems to have been interested in architecture from an early age, when English Palladian taste was very much in vogue. He was certainly fascinated by Parisian architecture during his time there. His enthusiasm for the Hôtel de Salm, a charming house on the river, with a circular salon inserted centrally into the rectilineal block of the house (now the headquarters of the Legion of Honor), is on record. And he consulted Charles-Louis Clérisseau, who had worked with Robert and James Adam (and whom he knew in Paris) on the design of the Virginia Congress, basing the building on the Maison Carrée in Nîmes, the best preserved Roman building in France.

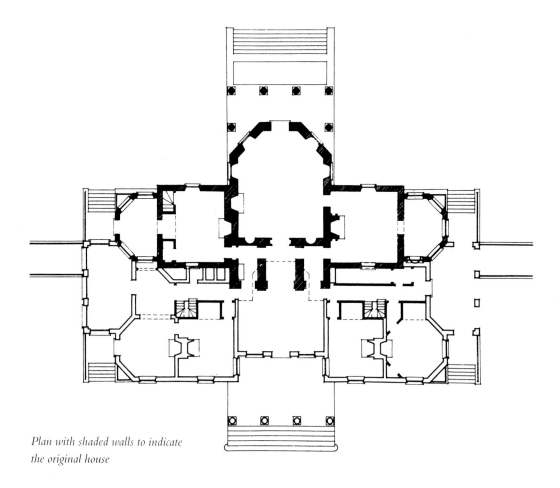

Plan with shaded walls to indicate the original house

The house he built for himself accommodated his considerable personal library, which included much professional literature. Although Jefferson was no great draftsman and used squared paper for his measured drawings, he was a passionate student of architecture and craftsman enough to execute some of the work on his house – as he would later labor on the models of his mechanical inventions. It is clear that he designed and redesigned his home at Monticello over the course of many years. He built the first, smallish house about 1770, deriving much of it from English pattern books, especially those of James Gibbs and Robert Morris. When he returned from Paris he enlarged the house greatly and made it more refined and complex.

The proportions of the house are governed by two Roman Doric porticoes, one on the east or entry front, one on the west or garden side. The entry columns were preserved from the old house. The most conspicuous addition to the original building is the domed garden front. Although the octagonal dome is such a prominent feature of the configuration, it does not correspond to any important chamber within. The only double-height room is the rectangular entrance hall, which contained the private museum. The stairways are tucked away in corner passages. The parlor, which was the main social center of Monticello, is under that dome, but is not octagonal; it is a rectangle with a huge bay looking out onto the gardens. Over the parlor is an octagonal domed room whose use is not clear in spite of its prominence.

The house extends symmetrically into lower out-buildings – kitchens, smoke rooms, cellars, garden sheds – which do not look out onto the garden, since the grounds are on the brow of the hill. All were connected to the house by underground passages. As for the garden, Jefferson had the lawn enclosed by a serpentine path edged with variegated borders and oval flower beds.

Jefferson was wildly enthusiastic about mechanical invention, and Monticello includes all sorts of technical ingenuities: the bed, which doubles as a storage space, one of the earliest polygraphs, as well as various timepieces are on display. Service in the dining room was dependent on a number of dumbwaiters.

Upper vault

Karl-Friedrich Schinkel # Schloss Glienicke

Berlin, Germany, 1825–c. 1837

The Prussian royals were keen on architecture. Not, oddly enough, Frederick the Great (who liked rococo, but was mean to his builders), but both his rather philistine father and his great nephew, Frederick William III. The king was an architect himself but recognized the genius of a most brilliant subject, Karl-Friedrich Schinkel (1781–1841). The destruction of the Berlin Wall has contributed in part to the increased interest in his work, since a large number of his completed buildings lay east – either in or close to Berlin – in the former German Democratic Republic.

The Palais or Schloss at Glienecke was rather abandoned during the Cold War, standing as it did just by the armed bridge that was used as the exchange point for spies and hostages; it is a miserable metal bridge that replaced an earlier stone one designed by Schinkel as part of the Glienecke layout. The diminutive palace was begun in 1825 for Prince Karl Friedrich, the younger son of Frederick William II, and a keen (if amateur) archaeologist and collector of antiquities. The architect, Karl-Friedrich Schinkel, was himself a keen antiquarian and used the little palace, but above all the various garden buildings, to experiment with ideas about the wooden origins of ancient architecture as well as the use of gilding and polychromy. At the highest point of the hilly site stood a circular belvedere, also known as the *Grosse Neugierde* or the Great Inquisitiveness, from which there was a splendid view of the lake; and Schinkel disposed the walks about the pavilions and fountains, using the level changes with great cunning, and balancing open views against enclosed stairways. The palace itself was deliberately underplayed, its lowly proportions giving more importance to the fountains and ornamental pavilions around it. The main residence was articulated into palace, casino (which also overlooks the lake), and elaborate outbuildings (which decentralized the palace park).

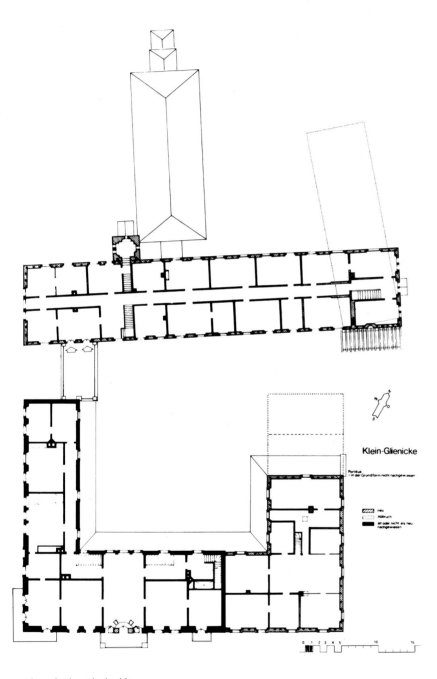

Klein-Glienicke

Plan of Glienicke buildings

Christian Gottlieb Cantian, granite bowl

Following pages: Formal approach with the Fountain of the Two Lions, which was added in the 1840s

*A chapel-pavilion in the garden,
by an architect after Persius, possibly
Heinrich Strack*

Ludwig Persius, exedral bench, c. 1840

Detail of the garden facade

Schinkel was born in 1781 in Neu-Ruppin, a small Brandenburg village. Following his father's death in 1795 the family moved to Berlin. His decision to become an architect seems to have been aroused by a display of Friedrich Gilly's plans for the Friedrichsdenkmal, the memorial to Frederick II the Great of Prussia, and he entered the school run by Gilly senior. The younger Gilly died at the age of twenty-eight, leaving behind drawings and influential writings. Schinkel saw himself as a Gilly disciple and sought to extend and interpret a sadly curtailed life.

Schinkel soon joined the Prussian building authority (the *Königliche Technische Ober-baudeputation*), of which he eventually became director. He was asked by the king to design the Neue Wache on Unter den Linden, and then the museum (better known today as the Altes Museum), both in the center of Berlin, as well as interiors for the royal family at Charlotten-burg, the Kronprinzen palais, operatic sets, mausolea, picture frames, even medals (notably the Iron Cross). His output was prodigious.

The "Grosse Neugierde" (Great Inquisitiveness), 1835–37

<small>Adolf Loos</small> # Villa Karma

Montreux, Switzerland, 1904–6

Theodor Beer was a rich man and a reputable scientist, as well as professor of comparative physiology at Vienna University. He bought a small house and piece of land on Lake Geneva, near Montreux, and contacted Adolf Loos (1870–1933) about rebuilding the existing structure. In 1903 Loos was the best-known (though not particularly experienced) architect in Vienna. It is not clear how he and Beer met, but both were contributors to the *Neue Freie Presse*, and Beer approached the project experimentally. He had clear ideas about what he wanted, and the relationship was not smooth. Moreover, while work on the house was progressing, Beer was accused of sexual abuse. He left Vienna, first for Switzerland, then for America, and wrote a number of times to Loos from Chicago and San Francisco, exhorting him to leave his wretched Balkan corner (he meant Vienna) and move to the great American spaces: he thought Loos would design marvelous luxury cars for Pullman!

Beer urged Loos to encourage his intellectual friends to agitate in his favor. And they did so. In spite of that, Beer was arrested on his return to Vienna, deprived of his university post, and sentenced to three months in jail. But he was financially independent and could retire to Montreux to pursue his scientific interests, as well as his concerns with Buddhism – hence the villa's name.

Loos did not need Beer's prodding to come to the United States. In the words of his biographers, his visit to the Chicago World's Fair of 1893 had been as important as Pacific travels were for Darwin. Brought up in Brünn (present-day Brno in the Czech Republic), he trained in Dresden before setting out on what was then an unusual venture for a young architect. It was a

time of architectural ferment. Daniel Burnham had undertaken to create an exhibition that would exceed the scale of the Paris one of 1889 by a factor of four, and it provided a showcase for the work of Louis Sullivan and others. Loos was enthralled, and his wonder grew as he reached New York City several months later. He settled in what was then Dutchtown, on Manhattan's Lower East Side, and survived as best he could, working in small sweatshops, in restaurant kitchens, and as a joiner before being appointed a draftsman in a small office. He returned to Vienna by way of London and Paris, though the impact of these two cities was more muted. At any rate, once home, he was absorbed into the circle of poet and critic Karl Kraus, and composers Arnold Schönberg and Alexander von Zemlinsky, a world of coffee-

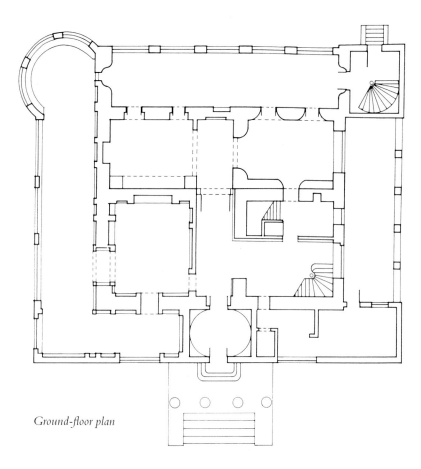

Ground-floor plan

Main facade

house discussions in which architecture figured a lot. Otto Wagner, who had dominated Viennese architecture in the generation before Loos, had published *Modern Architecture* in 1894, much of which had to do with the function of the building and truthfulness to materials, "The unpractical can never be beautiful."[1] Loos, about the same time, announced his psychological theory of architectural ornament:

Our age cannot invent ornament, it can only borrow it. We may appropriate historical motifs, such as classical columns, and use old furniture and carpets,

but what we make anew must be smooth and clean. Our very own ornament is the beauty of materials, particularly smooth ones: leather, silver, polished stone.[2]

Villa Karma is a perfect realization of Loos's theory, even though he was never quite able to finish it because of the problems mentioned above; the bulk of the later work was done by Max Fabiani, one of Wagner's most brilliant pupils, and finished by Hugo Ehrlich, another Dalmatian friend of Loos. It is now difficult to establish who exactly did what, but Loos can certainly be credited with the main organiza-

1. Otto Wagner, *Modern Architecture: A Guidebook for His Students to This Field of Art*, introduction and translation by Harry Francis Mallgrave (Santa Monica, Calif.: Getty Center for the History of Art and the Humanities, 1988).

2. Burkhardt Rukschcio and Roland Schachel, *Adolf Loos, Leben und Werk* (Salzburg: Residenz Verlag, 1982).

Library

View of the oval entrance hall from the second story

tion of the exterior: new buildings wrapped around the old shell and framed between two towers crowned by pergolas. The terrace formed by the roof of the addition opens out to the lake, while the dour road facade is prefaced by a Doric porch. Though this is usually thought of as Beer's own contribution, Loos loved the Doric column and had even proposed to build one twenty-two stories high as an office for the *Chicago Tribune*.

In the interior of Villa Karma, marble is pervasive: the oval, double-height entrance hall is panelled in red and yellow marble and vaulted with mosaic; the master bathroom is columned and panelled in black marble; the dining room has marble walls and a copper ceiling; the library bookshelves are framed with marble (though this may not have been determined by Loos) and they contrast rather splendidly with the wooden ceiling. The juxtaposition of rich materials, the skillful management of an awkward plan, the equally ingenious filtering of light, and the use of reflective surfaces all witness to Loos's presence at Villa Karma.

Entrance hall, view to ceiling and skylight beyond

Upper level of the entrance hall

Marble bathroom

Dining room

Le Corbusier # Villa Savoye

Poissy, France, 1929

The son of a Swiss watchmaker, Charles-Edouard Jeanneret (1887–1965 – he took the name Le Corbusier in 1920) spent all his working life in France. He was born in La Chaux-de-Fonds, where he attended an arts and crafts school and was first trained as a watch designer. He began designing buildings as a teenager in his home-town, and then traveled frequently to Paris, Munich, and Berlin, where he, like Ludwig Mies van der Rohe, was to work for Peter Behrens. After the war he moved to Paris for good, founding a new art movement, Purism, with the painter Amédée Ozenfant, for whom he designed a studio house in 1922; it was virtually the first concrete, plain, but carefully proportioned house in what was to become the man-ner most associated with him.

The Villa Savoye is named after its owners, who commissioned it in 1929 as a weekend country house. The clients, Le Corbusier said, had no design preconceptions, stylistic or otherwise, but owned a splendid, wood-girt site at Poissy, to the northwest of Paris. Although Le Corbusier thought of the Villa Savoye as a house of universal validity, which could be put down in any surroundings, it did look particularly well on the green lawns of Poissy.

The observant visitor will note first the triple division of the house: the glazed ground floor; the horizontally opened *piano nobile,* or *corps de logis,* set on columns or *pilotis;* and the airy, curvaceous, unusually tall and windowless attic. The ground story is withdrawn, its curve following the minimum turning circle of a car at the time. It contains a garage for three cars, a laundry room, and three servants' rooms. A car may be driven in underneath, through the columns, which hold up the first floor and form a porte-cochère. The outer point of the curve has the front door, which leads into a large hall. From this point a staircase and a ramp – which is the spine of the house – ascend. Between ramp and staircase, rather strategically placed, a freestanding pedestal washbasin is an invitation to the visitor to cleanse him- or herself before making the ascent on that ramp – perhaps the first time it has been made such a prominent feature of a private house. As Le Corbusier insisted, this house can only be appreciated by walking through it. *Promenade architecturale* is a term he coined, and the Villa Savoye seems almost designed to explain what this essential idea meant to him.

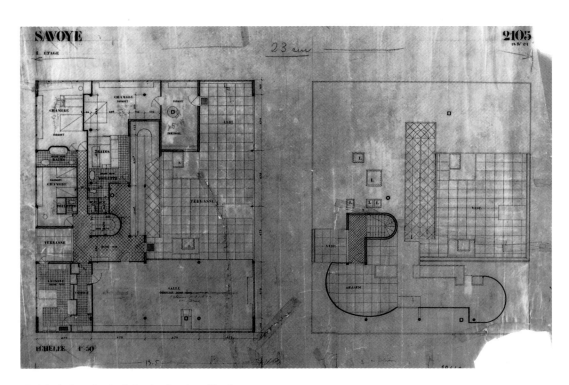

Original plans for the living level and roof level

Spiral stair

Preceding pages: East view

Central ramp

The principal floor is laid out generously around an open courtyard, of which the ramp is a striking feature. Large rooms – three bedrooms, each with its bathroom (one of which has been copied in a Hollywood house), and a long living room, kitchen, and pantry – have the same horizontal windows overlooking the green meadow and woods. Above that is the tall windscreen of the attic: two curved walls linked by a straight one, painted a warm color outlined against the blue (or gray) of the sky and providing the owner with a retreat and a belvedere appropriate to a villa.

In contrast to fellow "stars," such as Mies or Walter Gropius, Le Corbusier remained in France throughout World War II and was therefore well placed to play a role in reconstruction after 1945. But the Villa Savoye had suffered much, having been abandoned by its owner and used as a lumber store during the war. In the years directly following the war a particularly graceless and very institutional secondary school was built nearby, blocking its views. However, André Malraux, Charles de Gaulle's culture minister, declared it a national monument; since then it has been – not very faithfully – restored. But one of its main treasures, the view, is lost for good.

Preceding pages: Terrace and roof

Terrace

Bathroom

Corridor on living level

Frank Lloyd Wright # Fallingwater

Mill Run, Pennsylvania, 1934–37

The beginning of the 1930s was a low point in Frank Lloyd Wright's fortunes. The stock market crisis meant a hiatus in building. He was sixty, and his stance as the lone genius pitted against the "mobocracy," an uncomprehending and philistine society, did not endear him to clients. He was also reputed to experiment both formally and technically at the expense of his clients to a degree seldom allowed another architect. He was, however, a remarkable, if sometimes intuitive, structural engineer as well as a designer.

Fallingwater was designed and built as a week-end house for a Pittsburgh department-store magnate, whose son had been a student of Wright's and went on to become a distinguished architectural historian; he tells the story of his father's first consultation with structural engineers on Wright's drawings. They were convinced that the parapets were a dead weight on the terraces, as is usually the case, and would not accept Wright's use of them as edge beams instead. They declared the house unbuildable. Wright replied by putting their letters in a metal box, and set them into one of the walls of the finished house, which was built as a series of terraces over three stories, cantilevered out of a stone core that goes down to the bare rock and acts as a counterweight to the long projections. They achieve their most spectacular effect on the main floor, where the huge living room opens out to even larger terraces with steps down to a pool formed by the cascade.

Having inspected and surveyed the site, the clients expected a project that would face the waterfall; what they got instead was a house terraced *over* the waterfall. This was a decision based on Wright's understanding of the American landscape. One aspect of what he called his organic architecture was that it should not intrude on the site, but appear at one with it,

seeming to grow out of it. That situation has given the house at Mill Run in Pennsylvania its name and its extraordinary fame. Its construction seems to have turned Wright's luck. The S. C. Johnson & Son Inc. Administration Building in Racine, Wisconsin, was built in 1936–39, and there followed a whole series of splendid houses, including, in 1939, a guest-house for Fallingwater.

Wright (1869–1959) was born of Wisconsin-Welsh stock but moved early to Chicago. He worked for Louis Sullivan, whom he always acknowledged as his master. He came into contact with Japanese architecture, and indeed many of the motifs that would recur in his designs – the sliding screens, the deep overhangs, the low platforms – may have been inspired by the interest in the manner that was also prevalent in Europe at that time. But he was also very small – just over five feet; this conditions Fallingwater's wide overhangs and once prompted him to say that had he been six inches taller the history of western architecture would have been different. A six-foot-three friend of mine finds Fallingwater acutely uncomfortable. Fortunately, Wright's clients were not very tall and until the family died out, leaving the house to a trust as a landmark, it was their villa and retreat.

View from the south

Following pages: View from the northeast

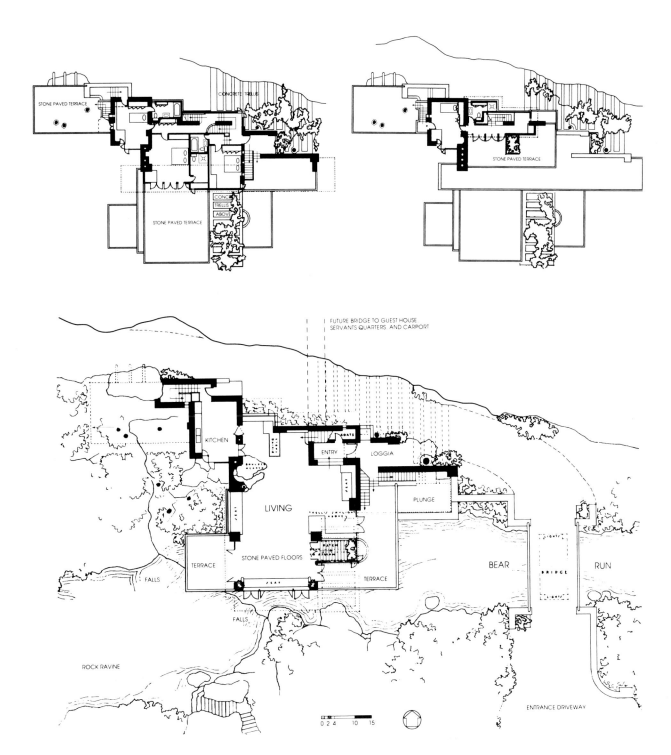

Plans of the main, second, and third floors

View from the northwest

Living room, detail of access to the open stair

*The open stair leads from the living
room to a platform above the waterfall*

The open stair

Living room

Living room, with fireplace, viewed
from the dining area

Dining area

A corner in the third-floor bedroom,
with built-in desk and shelves

Hallway

Ludwig Mies van der Rohe # Farnsworth House

Plano, Illinois, 1945–51

Ludwig Mies van der Rohe (1886–1969) left Germany in 1937, having realized that he could make no accommodation with the Nazis, and that his past (he had, for instance, designed the memorial to Karl Liebknecht and Rosa Luxemburg, the left-wing leaders murdered in 1919) had turned him into a marked man. In any case, his extremely sober modernity was unacceptable to the Nazis. He took up an invitation to Chicago, and in 1938 became the director of the Armour (later Illinois) Institute of Technology.

He was already very well known internationally. Born in Aachen, the son of a mason, he moved to Berlin in his early twenties and entered the offices of first Bruno Paul, and later Peter Behrens, one of the most important figures of the twentieth century, for whom Walter Gropius and Le Corbusier (very briefly) had also worked. Behrens had been invited by Mrs. Kröller-Müller, a famous art collector, to design a house to include a gallery for her collection. The project dragged on, and she then invited Mies, as the assistant in charge, to come to The Hague and supervise the building, of which a full-size wood-and-cloth model had been made. That was in 1914 and World War I would soon put an end to that scheme. Meanwhile Mies had done his first independent houses and, after 1918, he was responsible for a series of brilliantly conceived and drawn projects for glass and concrete skyscrapers. In 1925, the year of the monu-

ment to Liebknecht and Luxemburg, he became first vice director of the Deutscher Werkbund, and the planner (and part executant) of revolutionary housing in Stuttgart, the Weissenhof Siedlung, for which his old boss Behrens, as well as Mart Stam, J. J. P. Oud, Gropius, and Le Corbusier all designed buildings. Mies himself designed a long block of apartments for it, in which the internal space was free of structural impediments (the walls were movable), while color was used to emphasize volumes. Then there were his two most famous spare and uncompromising buildings: an exhibition pavilion for Germany at the Barcelona International exhibition in 1929, and a house for the Tugendhat family in Brno, Czechoslovakia, in 1928–30. On the Nazi seizure of power in 1933, he took over as director of the Bauhaus in Dessau, but was soon compelled to move the school to Berlin. It was closed down in 1935.

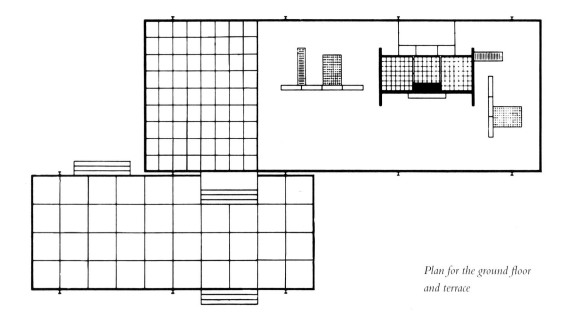

Plan for the ground floor and terrace

Approach from the south

In Chicago work initially came slowly, but then in huge quantities. IIT had him working on buildings almost as soon as he was appointed to the faculty. In addition, Edith Farnsworth asked him to design a house in the country for her. It was his first realization of a structure entirely supported from the outside: a floor and a roof slab are held nine and a half feet apart by two rows of steel columns. This was floodable land, so the raising of the floor had its rationale. All the welded joints were sand-blasted and the whole structure painted. The interior space is articulated rather than divided by a "service unit," while two bathrooms separated by closets make an oblong rectangle; the kitchen is on one long side, a figured or inherently patterned wood surface on the other. The figured wood, the travertine floor, and

the raw silk hangings exemplify Mies's motto, "Less is more" (later rejected by another generation, who decided that "less is a bore").

The Farnsworth house has the concentration of minimal luxury with leisure, which gives the concept of the villa a particularly twentieth-century twist. After this domestic venture, Mies's role in the transformation of the twentieth-century city was perhaps greater than that of any other architect, even though his message has been very misunderstood. His lean, austere, almost scientifically precise structures have been much copied the world over, but whereas he has always known how to achieve his effect by the most elegant means, in other hands his approach often descends to the soulless and the tawdry.

North facade

West facade

Gwathmey Siegel & Associates Architects # François de Menil House

East Hampton, New York, 1979

Charles Gwathmey (b. 1938) was one of the original New York Five, the "white architects," who bound themselves to follow a strict formal discipline and loyalty to the kind of architecture that goes by the name "International Style" in New York. He and Robert Siegel (b. 1939), his partner, have been responsible for many institutional buildings, most famously the controversial addition to Frank Lloyd Wright's Guggenheim Museum in New York, as well as the Science, Industry and Business Library for the New York Public Library, and the museum-library addition for the Fogg Museum at Harvard. While the Gwathmey Siegel buildings may seem more relaxed than some of their "white" colleagues, they have kept faith with the method.

The house at East Hampton was designed for
François de Menil, a young art collector who
later became an architect himself. It stands on
the East Hampton dunes, and is entered from the
north, past a stuccoed entry pavilion (which
has a caretaker's lodge) along a cobbled drive.
This runs by a lake and a tennis court to the
forecourt of a vertical cedar-sided house. It stands
on a wide terrace of green slate, and inside are
polished black granite floors. The slate podium
extends westward to accommodate a swimming pool and its terrace. The internal built-in
woodwork is in polished mahogany, and these
materials – together with the white metal-
work and window frames – provide the coloring of the house. The interior walls are also
cedar sided.

The house's main entrance is through a porch
that is two stories high and cuts into the first
layer of the house. The whole building is
thought of as a series of such layers. Most of

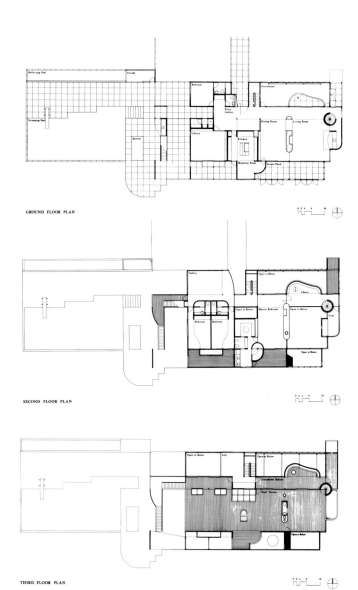

GROUND FLOOR PLAN

SECOND FLOOR PLAN

THIRD FLOOR PLAN

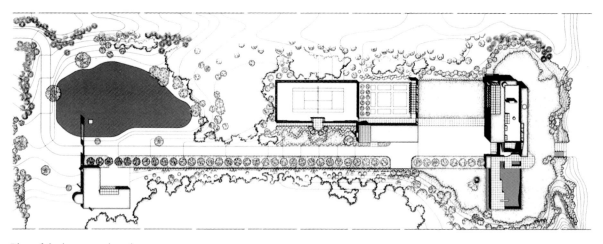

*Plan of the house, pool, and
surrounding grounds*

Pool and west elevation

*Preceding pages: North facade,
with main entrance*

the first one is taken up by the north-facing greenhouse that rises through the whole height of the house, and projects over the roof, so that it becomes a beacon at night.

Much of the play of the house is in the section, with other spaces rising through all three floors. Beyond the circulation area is the zone of the living room and bedrooms; all of them face south into the fourth zone, which is a deep *brise-soleil*, a porch that again rises the whole height of the house – like the colonnades of southern colonial mansions – and so offers a shaded outlook from the roof deck onto the dunes and the ocean. The west end of the house overlooks the swimming pool, dissolving into an interplay of decks and stairways, which makes an enthralling climax.

View from the southwest

View from the third floor

Southeast elevation

*Preceding pages: Detail of the southwest
end of the house*

Triple-height glassed-in porch

<small>Richard Meier and Partners</small> # Neugebauer House

Naples, Florida, 1998

The New York architect Richard Meier (b. 1934) reached the greatest international recognition with the achievement of the Getty Center, the cultural complex that crowns a hill overlooking the San Diego Freeway in north Los Angeles. The Getty showed his unique capacity for uniting very different building programs into a satisfying whole. Of course, his earlier work already included a number of public commissions throughout the world – in Paris, The Hague, Frankfurt, Ulm, Barcelona, and Rome. Yet he has always concerned himself with the private dwelling, of which the recent waterside house built in Naples, Florida, is an outstanding example.

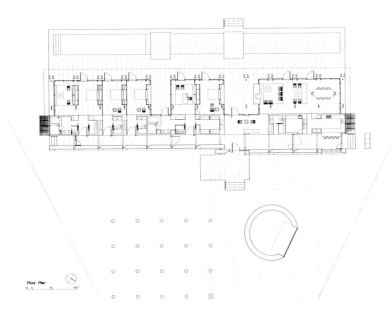

Plan of the house, garage, and palm grove

West facade

The Neugebauer House is a villa of a different type than others featured so far in this book, if only because it is the only one that directly overlooks the open water, like Pliny's Laurentine villa. This long bar of a house, three by one in proportion, faces Doubloon Bay. It is approached through a regular five-by-five square plantation of Florida palms, over a grassed but reinforced surface that allows for both pedestrians and drivers. The palm grove is balanced by a low cylinder of a garage on the other side of the entrance, which is marked by a platform projecting on the grass. The house turns its back to the road with a limestone wall pierced by thin lancet windows that screens a continuous passage running the whole length of the house. This spine gives access to a range of bedrooms and living rooms, a buffer zone of bath and service rooms, as well as the kitchen. It is broken once by the wide, deep entrance porch. The striking rhythmic, syncopated effect of the wall is emphasized by the way in which – unexpectedly – the boxed rafters, which carry the glazed and low-pitched roof, perch next to the lancet windows to create a strong shadow-play, while the beam that carries them is concealed by the thickness of the wall.

The visitor enters the house by stepping up to the porch, which is an embrasure in the volume of the house, not a separate structure; beyond this the house is laid out on one level. This entry porch leads first into the foyer and then through to a wide back porch, which opens to the lagoon. On this side, another platform and a reflecting lap pool run the whole length of the building, providing a hiatus between the formality of the house and the untamed beach, while augmenting the luminosity of the interior.

The tonic, restorative effect of water and sun is celebrated by the very structure of the house, and is particularly striking on the bay front. The butterfly construction, which interprets the local demand that all roofs be pitched, is low to the entrance, high toward the sea, to which the whole house opens. This roof, which stands on box-stanchions, is covered by reconstituted stone panels that are like huge shingles. The south facade is double: the outer screen is a *brise-soleil* frame connected by a horizontal canopy to the glass facade, so as to introduce a low, fully shielded clerestory under the butterfly roof. It also contains a system of blinds. The *brise-soleil* literally breaks the direct sunlight by a curtain of closely set aluminium rods that allow the shimmer of the sun to stray within.

West facade and the pool

*East facade and the garage,
viewed through a palm grove*

Southwest view

East facade and the garage

Index

W

Z

Credits